A Reader's Guide To Time

Rebecca Cullen

Dear Barbara —

I love your hound mourn
and I'm looking forward to
hearing much more
howwowling.

lots of love

Becky x

First Published in 2022
by Live Canon Poetry Ltd
www.livecanon.co.uk

978-1-909703-53-7

A CIP catalogue record for this book is available from the British Library.

Rebecca Cullen has a PhD in Creative and Critical Writing. She was the second poet-in-residence at Newstead Abbey, ancestral home of George Gordon, Lord Byron. Director of the Writing, Reading and Pleasure (WRAP) extracurricular programme at Nottingham Trent University, Rebecca also curates and presents the Notts TV Book Club.

Acknowledgments

Thanks are due to the editors of the following publications in which versions of some of these poems have appeared: *The North*, *PN Review*, *New Poetries VII* (Carcanet) and *Ink, Sweat and Tears*. Special thanks to Ann and Peter Sansom at The Poetry Business for their inspiration of many kinds – and for publishing some of these poems in *Majid Sits in a Tree and Sings*.

Contents

Subjective Time ('of our lives')

Poetic Time (also 'of Reading')

Deep Time

Cyclical (also seasons, see 'Calendars')

Quantum

For D.J.S. and J.R.M.S.

Prologue

It's not place which interests me. When everything is strange and different perhaps writing comes more easily. Go somewhere, see something, write something down. I've walked the same routes, the same days of the week, the same months in different years.

Try seeing the same thing, for years and years. Cry or dance on the same street when you are sixteen and twenty-seven and forty-five. Try seeing spring differently, so that the fiftieth time you see the same cherry trees, they are as fresh and new as that first hazy glimpse.

I sit on the same bench in 1973, and 1982, several times in 1997, last year, but the bench and I have always been the present. When I look at the bench, I see all those nows. When I sit down, those presents converse. Here there is no distinction between past, present and future. I walk it, taking all my people with me.

Consider time. The way it collects and stays. The way it transforms place to make it look different and the same, the way it moves and binds and rests. I love the layer upon looping layer. Thick and impenetrable, difficult to climb over or circumvent. Time is gritty in the air.

Don't say it. Let it bend, dissembling and blurring the past and present, leaping backwards from the future. Put yourself in time, not place. Play like this so you don't when you are.

It's time I love, winding as a cat wraps round an ankle.

Narrative Time (myths, legends)

The Enigma

When science failed them,
they turned to cromniomancy
and when the store of winter onions
was depleted, they dyed feathers,
wedged them in roof crevices
to observe the sequence
of the scatterings.

They chose a bleating kid,
cut out its heart; realising then
the gods' desertion,
they cast teeth, sent offerings
to the hermit of the woods.

A fact-finding expedition
crossed the wetlands
on a train of camels,
found nothing but a thick
waxy residue where his cave
had been. (Folklore reports
he wore a cape fashioned
from the skins of sacred snakes).

No one knew why or when
to expect a recurrence.
Their lives became a slim
horizontal passageway
through which no one came
and no one went.

Yes, this really happened.

The Gradual Loosening of Decorum

One bright morning, when overnight,
winds had driven winter from the place,
the bank manager arrived and found
the minute hand plunged through his window.

The council came to shift it
and the arrow made him think of being a boy,
of cowboy films and rolling yonder, yonder –
his dreams of eating beans around a fire.

He felt a yearning for the days before age
lay heavy on him, before the tally, and the column
and the safe. (Time was time and discipline
must be maintained).

Finally, they levered off the hour hand as well.
Children ambled on their way to school.
Everyone arrived, eventually,
though there was no time at all.

Once there were three clocks:
one outside the GPO; one at the High Street's end;
but the clock in The Square was the first to stop
no one can remember years ago.

Lark at the Dinner Party

They said it would take twenty minutes
from the Tube. She ascends, clutches
everything she needs this evening.

One stick of colour to slick her lips.
One coiled string of pearls to double
in her fingers, loop around
an unsuspecting neck.

Two pens – excessive in a bag this size.
Experience has taught her not to rely
on ink, that it oozes.

A while ago, the names of things deserted her.
The notebook is a place for all that loss.
Brother. Duct tape. Tarantula.

The gin inside the bag inside the bag.
Press the bell, Lark. Smile brightly.

How the Rock at Lizard Point Became

The storyteller says the hunt gathered at the summit,
pounded manacles from ice and ore. She stooped to drink
and heard them clatter; the pain behind her eyes was fear
and cold cupped palms of water. She took flight: flint
spray at her heels, wind-whipped, buckle-kneed
in downhill vertigo. They clanked and wailed across
the lakes and moors and chased her, reaching out for mother.
It ended where the earth meets the sea. When she had
no land left the hunt made haste to cast their chains.
She stepped into the water. Then the waves drew back;
her arm was petrified, a slip of shiny slate. She let
the waves fuss and hush her, make her stone, her long
neck streaked with seams of iron, a crease of green
for eyes, her hair behind, a fan of blood-red serpentine.

Crossing from Marazion

I am six when people first begin to stare —
a boy in man's clothing,
children leaping in my footsteps,
kite-tailing across the beach.

The mothers stand in doorways, trill
'He must wear his father's shoes!
What height will he reach full grown?'
We leave a single track.

At ten I anchor the village team
at tug of war. Then I join father
on the boat, learn to haul creels.
He says I am worth three men to him.

The Whit fair waltzes in
with whispers of the Show of Freaks.
The catch is bad. There is a curse.
My father's jaw sets firm.

That night, I see mother trawl her brow.
At low tide, she takes my hand
and we walk the causeway to the friars.

Joseph on Savile Row

His multicoloured coat is slightly faded now
but he stands behind the counter, all too
familiar with the bolts and brothers piling in
for wedding clobber. High spirited,
lubricated; they admire his vintage threads.

As he measures up the shoulder seams
he thinks of dreams, remembers lying
on Freud's couch, its worn dyed blanket,
the master smoking, stroking Jofi, jotting
notes on Moses, a fear of tribalism.

Majid Sits in a Tree and Sings

This morning, I wake with a bird in my heart.
My mother smiles only for me. I bash my car into the wall.
Sometimes she tells me to be quiet. Today, she laughs.

The men came in the hottest part of the day.
A walk, my love, a small walk, she says.
In the stairwell, the mothers hold their children.

The guns shine in the sun. I am a man,
this is no time for play, I do not hide.
We shuffle in, look for a seat in the stands.

A big black bird comes down from the sky.
The grown-ups hold their breath. They are blinking a lot.
The bird likes the meat hanging on the goalposts.

Tonight, my mother says I can sleep in her bed.
I make my back into a curved shell against her legs.
She strokes her palm across my forehead.

In the middle of the night, I watch her on her knees.
She tips her head backwards. I see all of her neck.

Women's Time (see also intergenerational, heroic)

Mother

Sometimes she is sick with new children, sometimes she is heavy with old ones. Panels hide cupboards stuffed with capes and muffs, stacks of dove-grey boxes. Panels hide balding dolls with wrists and ankles creased and fat. In a box, there are boots with wooden soles for babies. There are boots for babies, with wooden soles. The walls whisper things and promise. Her hands lie loose in her lap. Lace droops on her arm. Her door is closed to queues of questions. Her hands lie loose in her lap when they should be busy blanketing or running. Her cloth puckers at will, crumples; her palms are too hot, her fingers are too heavy. On the table, a pair of silver bird scissors, a pair of gold-rimmed reading glasses. There's a border she should be stitching, a border of a blue-winged fledgling. Her hands lie loose in her lap. She slips out a child every year from under her skirts, imagines every other baby crumpled in a brown paper bag. The walls whisper things and promise. There are boots for babies with wooden soles. There's a border she should be stitching. Her hands lie loose in her lap.

Opening

My shoes come sleeping in a box.
I hear them breathe inside the tissue paper book,
the sound of rippling leaves.

The sole is thick alright, like a slab of black tripe;
the toes are tapered and stopped inside,
adding another inch – at least – in length.

Who knows I spade my feet? Kick trees
until the bark flakes, then blame the deer?
Who knows I use my shoes to root?

These are wild shoes
with points like noses, keen like foxes,
the leather creased like ears.

Irresponsibility

After Shirley McClure

I'm not a house group leader anymore.
I don't miss typing up the schedule,
forgetting when people are at choir
and therefore, sadly, won't be able to attend,

or someone pointing out the timescales
are too tight. I don't miss pondering
discussion themes, which verse would most
support the person who is always early

and uses my home as a receptacle for complaints.
I don't miss knowing I'm an enabler
of their more exciting lives. I don't miss
thinking, yes, women are the family's sun,

but what happens when a rock has cracked
your solar panels, where does your help
come from then when you lift
your stinging eyes to the deaf heavens.

Picnics and Women in Sun

After Carl Sandburg

Let us drape our arms over the side of the rowing boat in summer, trail languid fingers in the weed and water, and let us talk of artists and teachers earnest in their studies.

Let us thresh the grass with tartan, spread our blankets — and talk about mothers and sisters wrapping sandwiches in paper.

Let us write of angry, hungry days, of rosettes, of sashes and women wanting votes, women called 'suffragette' making picnics in the sun, their underskirts flickering in newsreels, slipping under racecourse fences for women they did not know but loved.

Let us lie on our backs on our picnic blankets, our fingers touching, and remember Gudrun, in her emerald stockings, and Ursula, the heroine, and all the angry, hungry women who made picnics in the sun.

A feminist mother is only as good

as what she says to her barely teenage daughter
who has not been invited to a party.
In the muted syllables the mother holds
a pattern for the future.

The mother must not give the impression
the daughter was not wanted. She must waft
through a wildflower meadow of explanations:
the same primary; guestlist restrictions.

It's true the other mothers have been friends
for years. Their daughters can't be left
off the list instead. A feminist mother is only
as good as *girls can be cruel* kept in her head.

The Birthday

Walking to the cemetery, I see next door's new dog
asleep with his nose against the window.

The tree in the front garden is two weeks from a bud.
The snowdrops at its base have blown.

I'm not even sure which year it is. No one mows
a lawn or cleans a car, but all the cars are home.

At the bottom of the street, a young mother
crosses with a buggy. The flowers

crackle in the cellophane. We talk about
anything and everything. We talk about nothing.

Diving Swallow

There is no thrill like the thrill of a trapeze,
the acrobat with powdered soles, her feet
palming the rope ladder, each seventh rung
a pause for a tilted *port de bras*.

Patched up, taped up, a strapped-up knee
beneath the body stocking, still the same
vital statistics as the nineteen-year-old, just
two inches lower.

Intermittent sparkle on her sleeves, seams
on the brink; foundation cracked.
We have stopped colluding in this illusion,
fear in our thin-lipped mouths.

Tara

My hairdresser is young. She tells me
which way round the cape goes – 'like a coat'
and I stick my arms in like a scarecrow.

She asks me questions with dull answers.
I'm not going out tonight. We haven't booked anything yet.
What are the odds of reporting an occasion? Not high.

Tara's going to a party, then lazy shopping;
she might hang on for meatballs and lingonberry jam.
Her eyebrows are balanced between branch and twig.

She whisks the colour, listens carefully when
I bring up translucency, what a lack of oestrogen
might do to curls.

She got pregnant at 18. It sounds familiar.
Tara slathers on the Ash Brown and we're silent,
both thinking about roots.

Historical (n.b. timelines, clocks)

Paris, Grands Passages

To enter requires trust: you can't see the end
from the beginning. You can't see the next beginning.

Shop names are the contents page; each entrance
is a diorama. Post yourself into the future.

At Hotel Chopin, climb the three red stairs.
Would you like to buy a sink? A model of a carousel?

The tiles are monochrome and harlequin.
The gates can keep you out, or keep you in.

In the window of the *librairie*, two wax children
read a book, sitting in a rowing boat.

Claim a tall-backed chair at the café draped in vines,
warm beneath the glass roofs pinched like fish spines.

The taxidermist stitches swans' wings to a fox.
Come, watch the past play, hear your heels knock.

It was good to get away

She sat on the left side of the bus.
The last time her sister had reminded her
that Mother wasn't always easy.

She didn't have to do the nights
when the back door gaped,
when the woman who did not

know where she was, or who,
had somehow found the key
and quietly slipped into the garden,

where she stooped to foxgloves,
scooped the heads of peonies
in her cupped hands. She sighed.

Her stomach came undone when
she came up country. The roads
narrowed and wound. It was hard

to see what was around the corners –
just another stretch, a hairpin bend.
Once, a whole mile of pheasants

picked their way across the lanes.
The driver had to get down, shoo them.
Stupid birds. Such small brains.

The Picture his Son Carries in his Wallet

The first rests against a rake, shades his eyes under a hat.
A slim straw peeks from the corner of his mouth; his sleeves
are rolled up to the elbows, his shirt is slightly open.
There is a tear above the top pocket.

On his left is a boy with a cap, not old enough to shave
or for long trousers, grinning ear to ear, revealing his teeth
and the dimple in his chin. They both wear boots they sit
and polish in the evening, before setting them beside the fire.

Behind them, hay stooks stretch to the horizon.
It is the middle of harvest, the boy shrieking at his brother
to save the mice in the field, the brother telling him he's soft,
remembering the same thing, that day with his father.

Southbank

'I became my own obituary' — Jean-Paul Sartre, *Les Mots*

I took my usual route to the stalls between Southwark Bridge and Waterloo. I was after something short and French — poetry, perhaps. The sun seemed here to stay, on the heels of weeks of being undecided. I was due to start a job the following morning and for the first time since the war ended, I would have a salary. There was a breeze.

Although my brogues were thin-soled, I'd buffed them to a high shine. My hat was cheap, but it had a fetching brim. For a second, I imagined my survivors would retrace my steps, *Ah! This is where he walked and tried,* heard them speak kindly of my splutter of unimpressive arcs.

We'd been there time and time again — our heads inclined, a book divided on our upturned palms. And now we met; the river light molten in your hair. I hid my frayed tie in my sweater. You hold a water-marked Verlaine. I give myself away.

Chico Rico *el Payaso*

When he was a child, the world inside
his head was better than the world outside.
He was quiet at school. He loved the way
charm made the girls dip their eyes, coy
with delight. He wasn't good at sport,
was chosen last; they called him *el torpe*.
He heard a ball sucked into a palm on landing,
watched the fielders tilt – caught their gift
of timing. He observed his grandfather
extemporising, long fingers rippling
through the keys as he lay down the melody,
then destroyed it, then scooped it up.
He watched the tiny gymnast score a 10,
saw that practice finds perfection.
In bed he edged his radio dial, yearned
for who was hooting on the other side.
He learned to sing his sorrow like a lullaby.
And with not very many words,
he found us in the darkness, played out
our sadness, until he made us laugh.

When the taxi came –

it was the beginning of the end.
He dipped his head to take the weight
of the case curated for his family.

Dresses for his sister. Chocolates. Tea.
Gifts to show them 'British', the life
he'd learned.

At 4.32 she opened the back door and let
the world in. A budge down the stoop –
that case huge, large enough to hide her in.

They had imagined a lingering parting kiss.
He left. She lived on instant mashed potato.
She chased around the world for him,

but how do you find someone thirty years ago,
and who does he come back to when she's
not there, nowhere near the girl she was?

Joshua in St Mâlo

He stood legs akimbo, feet fully planted, about to launch into the Star-Spangled Banner, as if he'd landed for America. He told her his grandfather renamed himself Gold at immigration, said he was Columbus discovering Europe.

Here and now, the intergenerational fight for survival transported him to sleepy Brittany from Long Island, where each Christmas, visitors helped themselves to party bags of jewellery from two gigantic urns on his family's front porch.

They were both searching for the liberation of a fresh language. His French was *impeccable* – indistinguishable from his *langue maternelle*. She loved his love of the subjunctive, the way he sought out the politest ways of saying everything. A delight to hear him hitch-hiking.

Neither of them considered where they'd sleep. She'd imagined towers of *fruits de mer,* maritime-like carousing, but they had 12 francs between them, sharing *eau de Monoprix*; she should have known he didn't want his father to trace him through the credit card.

They made themselves have hunger by trading words for pancakes. At four her limbs slipped into the cleft between night and day, and she understood the etymology of blanched, anticipating sun on the ramparts, propped against his shoulders all the white night.

Subjective Time ('of our lives')

Michael

My mother's cousin,
an open book.
He adopted two children
in the seventies
and loved them.
One of them stopped
talking to him
in their teens,
but they were reconciled.

In my memory
he looks a bit like Johnny Ball,
a parent with enough enthusiasm
for the children of the nation,
enough to make them interested
in numbers, even,
when they wanted to be outside playing,
squirting water from cadged
washing-up liquid bottles,
wheedling *Can I have it yet?*
throughout the summer of 1976.

Michael had the knack
of smiling fresh each time
with warmth
and heartiness.

But what do I know
about heartache,
not having children,
of one your own and not your own,
the hope and prayer
that things will turn out right?

Sharon Moss in Three Acts

In the first, you lurk in the wings and in the orchestra pit.
You appear shortly before I win the prize then don't receive it;
you tell the judges that I stole the idea. You are immortalised
in my autograph book, writing
        'We sat on the greenest grass,
        the greenest we could find, but Beccy
        sat in something that a cow had left behind.'
You want to fight me when my arm is in plaster.
You spread my secrets, announce that I'm a bastard.

In the second, we are opposite each other on a tram.
I draw back into the seat to stop our knees from touching.
You're trim, your hair and the way your lips fasten neatly
over your teeth so you seem prim are still the same.
We chat and I am glad when you stand up and leave,
relieved to be shot of you. No one's called me my Sunday name
for years. I forget to pick up milk on the way home.

In the third, I am happy in a home when you move in.
I'm a size 12 but you bring them up to speed. I hear a rumour
I think I'm too good for them. I waste away and die
and you give the eulogy, say you always wanted to be the Pussycat,
you'd bought the tail and practised licking your hand like a paw.
But I was there, every time you thought you'd got the part,
the sympathy, the laughs. I didn't ever know how lucky I was,
that was my problem.

Special

Bring me *Too Much Too Young* on a portable in mono,
the summer in 1979 we walked *along the lonely street*,

not old enough for *NiteKlubs* or for beer that tastes *like piss*.
We wanted other bodies, pumping out their sweat,

digging their feet into the floor, stinking dirty dervishes
headed for a long *life without meaning* and *Threads* for dreams.

This is not nostalgia. We wanted to be older than we were,
to stay like that forever, to snog the fifth years

riding into school on scooters like in *Quadrophenia*,
wearing blazers, with their trousers taken in, throwing over

Forest for County to be more 2 Tone. It was the best
and worst of times, the honest blink before synthpop.

That was the next generation, with their clappy Thatcher
soundtrack, who don't remember gritted teeth to stop yourself

from crying for Yosser Hughes, his hungry kids. So
I won't dance in a club like this, where we are emotionally poor

with the whole world in our palms, where the children's
lunches come from foodbanks, where the government

dither and delay, *Do* absolutely fucking *Nothing*.

I take the coastal train from Norwich –

noticing the widening house-free gaps

between stations, and at West Runton
sit on a hillside with Steve, my destination,

who plays *Like a Hurricane* on his guitar
while I paint watercolours that make him laugh.

He's got a point. The sky, trees, heather and the sea
are already as they should be – and in any case

we haven't got the time to wait for paint to dry.
We laugh at everything that year, all through

the woods at the bottom of his garden, sending
cigarette smoke signals to our futures, whispering

6 Brunswick Street

Every afternoon now, we hear the clock
ticking down through next door's window.
We've pulled the sofa outside, our chairs
and cups. *Bring on the books* we shout;
John steps out with Beckett on his head.
We are speaking other people's words,
practising our bows. We are cramming
three years into our skulls, already
brimming with ourselves. One of Paul's
shoes is in the corner. He's lost the other;
it doesn't matter. We've been sunning
ourselves all May, all June. Barely clean,
completely looking, no one wearing shades.

15 April 1989

The house is in Broomhall, notorious. At this end,
there are terraces on both sides, descending
to tree-lined streets, broad flappy leaves.

It's a house for seven, our rooms
in different stages of disarray.
The red lino in the kitchen is never clean.

My room is the attic, which is a problem
for various reasons: visitors thud up
two flights of stairs – everyone bitches;

the loo; the skylight – the dark and cold
pressing. You think the glass will crack
and fall. When you're scared you light a candle.

You're in the middle of a short release final.
It's hot up there. The sirens start mid-sentence
and continue, until you realise they're closing in,

a flock of them, at the Hallamshire.
Two red teams in the semi of the FA Cup.
Easy easy for tragedy to slide in.

Sunday Call

It's hard to picture the post office
where you queue all day
to place your call.

Is it like the souks in films?
Is there a boy with a goat under his arm?
Are the women eating watermelon?

Here it rains all day.

I wait for the connection,
our careless talk without a grip.

If only I could blend
an essence of my words,
and send them down the line

to reappear in technicolour
at your end – or we had tins
and thread and hours to play.

Each call we learn no more, no less.

If you get through, I'm hot,
like I've been dragged on stage

And lost, because you laugh my name,
but I can't see you.

Pillar Box Dress

I come to you with no hope in my knees. We sit,
make the pub a confessional. Condensation slips
down the outside of my glass. We're here again:
same date, same table, same dress. Bonfire night
runs in the background, like a television on mute
during tea. We're talking in shrapnel. By the time
my drink is gone, your brother's waiting at the bar.
You say something about a spark. I stand, go home.

I don't leave drunken messages on your phone.
I play that song you never liked and sleep sprawled
across the bed. I keep my head. This much I know:
I'll change my hair, you'll be back by the New Year.
You're with the girl whose pout reminds you of Lolita.
In the morning, I fold the red dress and post it to her.

David

You are alone next to the greengrocer's,
hold forth while I clamp my punnet,
offer me the short or long story.

I want him back, to listen to your vamps,
your pauses, to recall our weave home
at four in the New Labour morning.

The last time I saw Trevor, he was a small boy
in old man skin, past caring about infection.
I kissed his excavated cheeks. I made him laugh.

This is loss, the way you sound the same.
I watch your feet brand the wet slabs.

My Father and I

Sometimes we didn't get on. The songs I sang
would please his ear. But I would over-act, embarrass him.

Now we go to appointments more often than we go for lunch.
After the last tests he couldn't be left alone. I spread across one sofa,

he slouched on his, and we watched a documentary on Howard Hughes;
I didn't know about the aviation or the Hollywood years.

So. We both kept turning up, not giving in.
Lately, I've taken to calling him daddy.

Poetic Time (also 'of Reading')

At the foot of Takhteshwar Hill
For Sujata

Green parrots with red beaks cruise
above the mango trees.

Are those mangoes ripe?
What kind of soil is best
for growing mango trees?

Sujata shows me how
to search the shade for snakes,
to tilt a rock for lizards,
to face that monkey, looking
straight into its eyes.

In the grizzling English winter,
these animals are metaphors
for waiting.

Today, we are standing in your poem
squawking at the crows.

Hey! Sujata!
Can you hear that panning camera?

The Inferences of Tengo and Aomame
After Haruki Murakami

I meet you at the top of a slide
    We look at two moons, your hand slipped in mine

You are not and every person in the crowd
    Twenty years since I last saw you: serious, unspeaking

That sniff, as the cap twists off a Coke
    I crouch in the clutter of your soul

We're linked by loss, a small gasp
    Perhaps it's dangerous

'I never had but one' or, The Significance of Boatswain

I think about the man and dog
rowing on the lake –
Byron diving in, giving Boatswain
the joy of rescuing him.

And Boatswain ill, his master
nursing him,
etching a poem for his friend,
its end '– and here he lies'.

And Byron ill, alone.
Where had his childhood gone?
Did he ever have one?
No reason then to stay –

no quickness bounding
down the steps to bark at hissing geese;
no barrel body on his chintz at night.

Just the coughing of his page.

Peacocks at Byron's Pile

I had a dream of Newstead Abbey,
that I was drifting through the garden
and the blowsy flowers were heavy on the walls.

The words are just ahead of me this morning,
the word for a large purple or white blowsy flower,
a climber, and a tree's branches so they grow

outstretched in two dimensions. *Espalier.*
Both these things are in my head, somewhere,
but the sparrows roost near the monk's pond,

which also has its own name,
and overlook the stump of oak on a lawn
where a raven has been adopted by two geese;

they are always in correspondence, everywhere
the remnants of a godforsaken kiss,
the three of them, like this. *Clematis.*

Nicole

'It's always a delusion when I see what you don't want me to see'
– *Tender is the Night*, F. Scott Fitzgerald

I'm waiting for my earrings to turn back to glass, tired of afternoons on the
terrace, the children's clamour for their father. This time it started when I
got the letter. The turned-up edges of the stamp left scalloped shadows. I sat
on the bathroom floor, the tiles veined like steak.

The letter was a lie and not a lie. I had watched the daughter lift her deep
brown eyes to my husband: a sin this side of the ocean. It was a kiss he'd
stolen. It was painful, but not irretrievable.

He found me with the letter in my hands, fluttering slightly, said it was the
letter of someone in the grip of mania. Nothing very new about that: after
all, he was my own writing cure.

To be clear, it was not the loops on the page, it was the way he made them
into madness. The wheel veering was no misjudgement, nor a mind sliding.
There was a cliff and a car. Shining is such a burden.

Women in Love

Endlessly in parlours, waiting in heavy silence
for the inevitable opinion, sentences repeated

when you're on the point of getting up
and doing something, wondering why yet again

you've been written into wittering on a swing
though in life you touch clouds with your toes,

while he stands with his moustache combed,
lip curled, buttoned up, hand on hip

as though rehearsing for an author photograph,
sucking it all in to spit out in the stories

you'll send in secret to a London publisher.
You know the price of fame is his forsaking you.

His brilliance rests on your secondary nature.
But you do it anyway, on the best notepaper,

writing of his industry and promise,
the way he's wasted in a stocking factory.

Your great heart and sacrifice
will bring him fame and bring you infamy.

So pluck gentians from the rockery,
red carnations from your décolletage

and batter them. Save up their petals,
make confetti you don't need and point

your life, your flame, in the direction
of your head, and over and over

pour out your gratitude for your escape,
his fecklessness.

'The Crossbys, she knew, were deeply resented'

Angela fell for Ralph as he stroked
his moustache, sluicing
a single malt around a tumbler.

It was hard to say why they were hated.
They flaunted no rules or regulations,
were polite and contributed in various ways.

Talk turned to
the flawlessness of their complexions
the cut and texture of their woollen suits
the shiny motorcar seen sidling in the lanes.

They had appeared, as if by magic,
in the spring of twenty-eight,
but no one really knew them.

Calder Thoughts

Then there was your carelessness with wives.
I love your wife – not as a saint or ghost
but for the mushrooms and the dizzy-making thumb.

This week I'm kipping at your house, the one you shared.
God forbid that I'm the ingrate guest. Your valley
is turning slowly back to branches

and I wonder where the leaves go, whether in the night
they've been inhaled and stratify the sky.
Some must drift into the river, turn to silt.

Next autumn, someone else may ponder this enigma,
sitting in the same chair, beneath the same sash window.
Keep this a secret. On the soft forest floor a fox stalks by.

Oh Joni

What have you done?
We're all floating on that river,
it has pinned us all to shame,
to skating away. The second

snow falls we're singing
songs of joy and peace.
They say you never wrote
a song which wasn't about you.

I'm here with the ghost of Sylvia,
thinking the same, almost,
about her. What a night
out that would be; Plath

and Mitchell with a guitar
and a sharp pencil. One
wholesome-looking blonde,
you swishing your flat hair.

The two of you sip cocktails,
swap stories of your many
and accomplished loves,
and when it comes, your

laugh cascades like a fountain
in the night. I recognise it
as I queue at the rank, the two
of you sidling into a taxi.

Deep Time

His Love of Newel Posts

There's a staircase in his memory
which in the present layers fear on fear.

A pillar of it rises from his feet
and spreads, so he's still

fixed there, wondering if
it's worth the risk of climbing,

eyes fixed on the ball
of wood he wraps his hands

around for safety. It's not what's
waiting at the top, it's what's behind.

There is no word for how he gets there.
Not tripping up the stairs because

he won't misstep; it's quick
like fingers through a scale,

pages in a flipbook, his elder cousins
playing snap. He's ascending,

he hasn't got a choice. Breath on
his neck, heels at his heels.

For the Record

1

---

[1] The lows are well-documented. Nights of rooms, the toils of repositioning. But dare we mention highs: the fecklessness; the noise; the relentless jape-making – the sprints through other people's lives, avoiding being touched? All limbs loose, all combinations of socks and colours, a bell sounding a bell sounding a bell on the right side of your brain. And the relief: to be completely lit, burning a path which is at once scorched earth and a route through a forest.

Night Fragment

He wakes her with a ball of sorry.
He wants her to hold it, keep it,
as brash and bold as the coin in her lungs.

His sob comes, warms her gut,
the flex of his young arm gone.

In the four o'clock light,
her face is crumpled, dirty.

Leaving London early to miss the traffic

Four boys shove
A Deliveroo driver
From a scooter and start to kick,
Drag the foodbox from his shoulders.
He rolls into a ball:

A hedgehog on a motorway
An early conker clinging to the white insides of its casing
A bubble just about to splatter
A semibreve on a stave
At the end of 'Rule Britannia'.

Confession

I forgot the birthday, then
remembered, but didn't send a card.

I said we'd go, we didn't. When I said
we would, I knew we wouldn't.

I left too soon, drank too much,
was miserly/lacking in affection.

I put luggage on the seats
all the way through London.

I cursed, gnawed my nails, bored my friends.
When you tripped, I grinned.

I broke my mother's plates, held a grudge,
lied, gossiped, stepped on someone else's toes.

I smashed a window, stole your socks,
talked over, contradicted.

I used the last of the milk then never owned up.
I bitched about all of the above.

I knelt on the beach wailing at the blank flat sky.
I thought I saw too much of you.

But that was the year

we stopped believing in years,
the year we thought would exemplify clarity,
the year we knew to be made of months
although a month turned out to be made
of years and then a day was made of years
and years were made of decades, and the decade,
well, the decade dug in its heels like a temporal
dodecahedron, like deserted platforms in the sea,
like latitude and very far away, like longitude
and stretching endlessly.

Cyclical (also seasonal, see 'Calendars')

These Winter Mornings

We stand on the porch and look down the avenue of facing houses,
their front yards and picket fences. Snow on either side.

A paperboy trudges where normally his wheels would fly,
a checked windcheater, a cap pulled low over his ears, a blue muffler.

He winds his way from house to house, mailing news into each mailbox.
We pause a moment, taking in the usual weather, then my husband turns

to lock the door and I freeze on the porch, opposite the tree-lined avenue,
the snow-tipped fences, the yards in front of each front door.

Someone will go to the trouble of putting on their boots, their coat,
their gloves and hat to slither for the paper.

I raise my arm to greet him. Paperboy shrugs,
pulls his windcheater tighter.

Spring Cleaning

I sit at my desk, watch a masterclass
in window-cleaning from the woman in the house
with a flagpole and Union Jack in the back garden.

She wipes the glass with a green duster before
polishing in circles, then takes a fresh cloth
and glides along the top and sides.

A hedge separates their house from Pat's.
The Council asked them to reduce it but they haven't.
Perhaps this is why when Mrs. Window's satisfied,

she draws the blinds. Mr. Windows likes a BMW,
has three cars on his drive. He's short and looks
as if he's never smiled. At Christmas they rickrack

a thick rope of neon across the front, mostly visible
from inside. She knows I'm watching, shuts
the curtains, then she peeks. I'm tempted to nod.
I've got my eyes on all the patriots.

February

February sits at the machine
with a tape around his neck.

Today, he's taking in the month.

A deep seam of concentration
pleats between his brows.

He tacks darts, removes
the pearl-headed pins,
drops them in a small
green bowl.

    They chink
like bells, heads heavy
like snowdrops.

February slides the soft
brown cloth beneath the foot
and clamps it, applies pressure
to the treadle.

    The fabric glides,
wheels through mud.

How to Hang Washing

It must be spring. There should be blackthorn
blossom, a smudge of sun across your cheek.

From your patch of earth, you'll hear the crest
of chatter from the playground at the school.

These pegs nip snugly, in time with magpie
calls, as your arms lift, stretch, clip, repeat.

Roost Articulations, Dusk

Please don't make me speak long, vast breath from my poor collapsing lungs:
don't make me speak. This is what I know is getting tighter in my throat,
    makes my insides crack.
The sounds are faster, faster – I have said as much as often. I wish I'd risen in the middle of the night you spoke
  and taken note of the small word 'ah', so miniscule and light, like a child
      singing to itself or speaking:
        two toy voices.
Then you said it, and for weeks I kept it close, could recall
   the phrase at will – but that's all gone now.
     The words are getting closer,
      you're making black fill all the gaps.
       There is no room and
        no remembering.
         Breath

      driven from my poor collapsing lungs.
This is what I know: tighter in my throat makes my insides crack; the sounds are faster;
   I have said as much as often as I wish. In the middle of the night
    you spoke: note of the small word, so miniscule
      and light,
       like a child singing to itself, speaking two toy voices.
        That's all gone now. The words are getting
         closer.
Don't make me speak breath from my lungs. Know is my throat.
My insides crack, the sounds are fast, I have said as much. In the middle of the night,
   note of the child singing to itself. You said, 'that's all gone.
    There is no room how you want it'.
      Breath from my lungs,
       my throat.
My insides fast. In the night, the child singing no room you want.
      Breath, throat.
       Child in the
        Night

         Singing

Walking with Richard

When we walk through town everyone looks at you.
To girls you're graceful, yet you worry your hair is too short –

this makes me laugh, like the time you wrote on Facebook
you had a nightmare where you woke up fat. On the bridge

boys eye you up. This happens every time we stroll
with no itinerary through different cities. Of all our walks,

you fitted Bloomsbury best: in Gordon Square
we zig-zagged up the stairs to find Virginia's Room.

You glide through library gates, dash last minute for your train,
your punctuality as artful as your cable knit, your pointed shoes

your fur-lined hoods. Where will all this walking end?
Once, in Birmingham, you said I'm your best friend,

which frightens me. You're bright and beautiful,
your legs are long, I'm often trying to keep up.

Each time I pass a Caffè Nero, I think of you.

Quantum

Douglas

Suddenly, he's eighty, wearing a mask
on his birthday and thinking of his girls
in well-respected places, wondering
if they're subverting the status quo
like him, turning the tables on those
who thought their brains were working
faster. They saw him striding across
campus and were mightily afeared.

Then the stages of experimentation
with facial hair; beards and whiskers,
ginger-tinged moustaches, sideburns
of different lengths, though never
in the fashion of Shane Fenton,
who he'd once seen emerging
from the back of a van in Ambergate.

Next, at Jack Taylor's gym, discovering
his feet and punches were too slow;
the story of his cousin, the lawn roller,
a dog, a hill and several fences. Finally,
he's eight, already wearing glasses. I watch
my dad like a mother, the spindly legs
I recognise, his face as he sits, crouched
beside the wireless, waiting for Zorro.

In the John Rylands Reading Room

After Gerard Manley Hopkins

I'm tired and drifting. Duns Scotus
in the stained glass leads me to Hopkins,
whispering, 'each day dies with sleep'.
It's a relief, like a lantern for a boat not quite lost.

I'm spent, but soon it will be spring.
The wheel-like weeds will shoot
lovely, long and lush. I'll watch hawks
sweep 'smooth on a bow-bend'.

And perhaps there is a budness to a bud,
a difference with precision: that which
each stem or wing doesn't have in common.
A pulse springing through all things, a rhythm.

Orlando

I was dry-mouthed in the Colosseum while you faced
the lions, and we read Classics and punted, and foiled
the mob and kept the diamonds. I wore your shoes
although they were too small for me, was your amanuensis,
and we owned a sweet shop, and a bookshop, and you were
the book I took out and kept, then lent and never got back.
We lived in frames opposite each other in the long gallery,
my breeches were plum velvet and you wore a clove
orange round your wrist, and we ached from quaffing
sherbet, and hid in the hollow of a tree. We were ravishing
on chaise longues brandishing gold-tipped cigarettes,
and hoofers drying out our stockings over the bath,
and boarders, in the same dorm, floating on our backs
after a midnight feast, in a natural pool filled by the tide.